It's A Beautiful Life
Sprinkles Publishing
England

"Lose Yourself In A World Of Color"

‹‹‹‹‹ scan this with your phone to win a free book!!

Sprinkles Publishing Co.
10 Lyndon Croft
B37 7EW
United Kingdom

Instructions:

1: Buy some nice pencils, gell pens or crayons.

2: Grab a chair or hit the sofa.

3: Pour a drink, wine if you can, soda if you like.

4: Get your favorite Sprinkles Publishing coloring book.

5: Put a blank sheet of paper under the picture you want to color.

6: Color in the picture.

7: Rinse and repeat.

P.S — Take a photo and show us, we will show the world your skills.

Calm alone time is your right as an adult. The more relaxed you become the better your life gets.

Hi, I know you have things going on today but could you do something for me? Leaving a review helps others find good coloring books and lets the world know how YOU feel about this one.

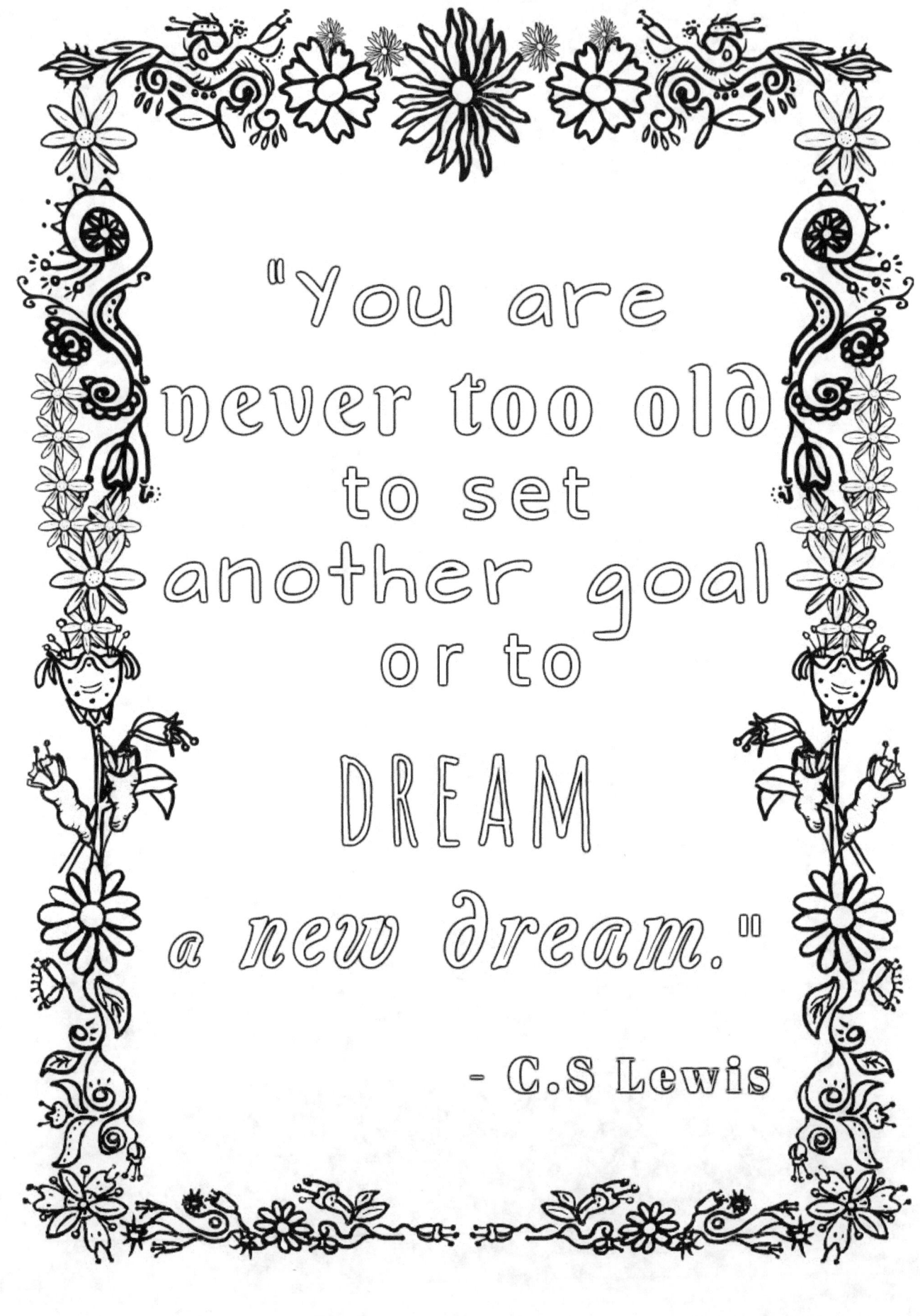

"You are never too old to set another goal or to DREAM a new dream."

- C.S Lewis

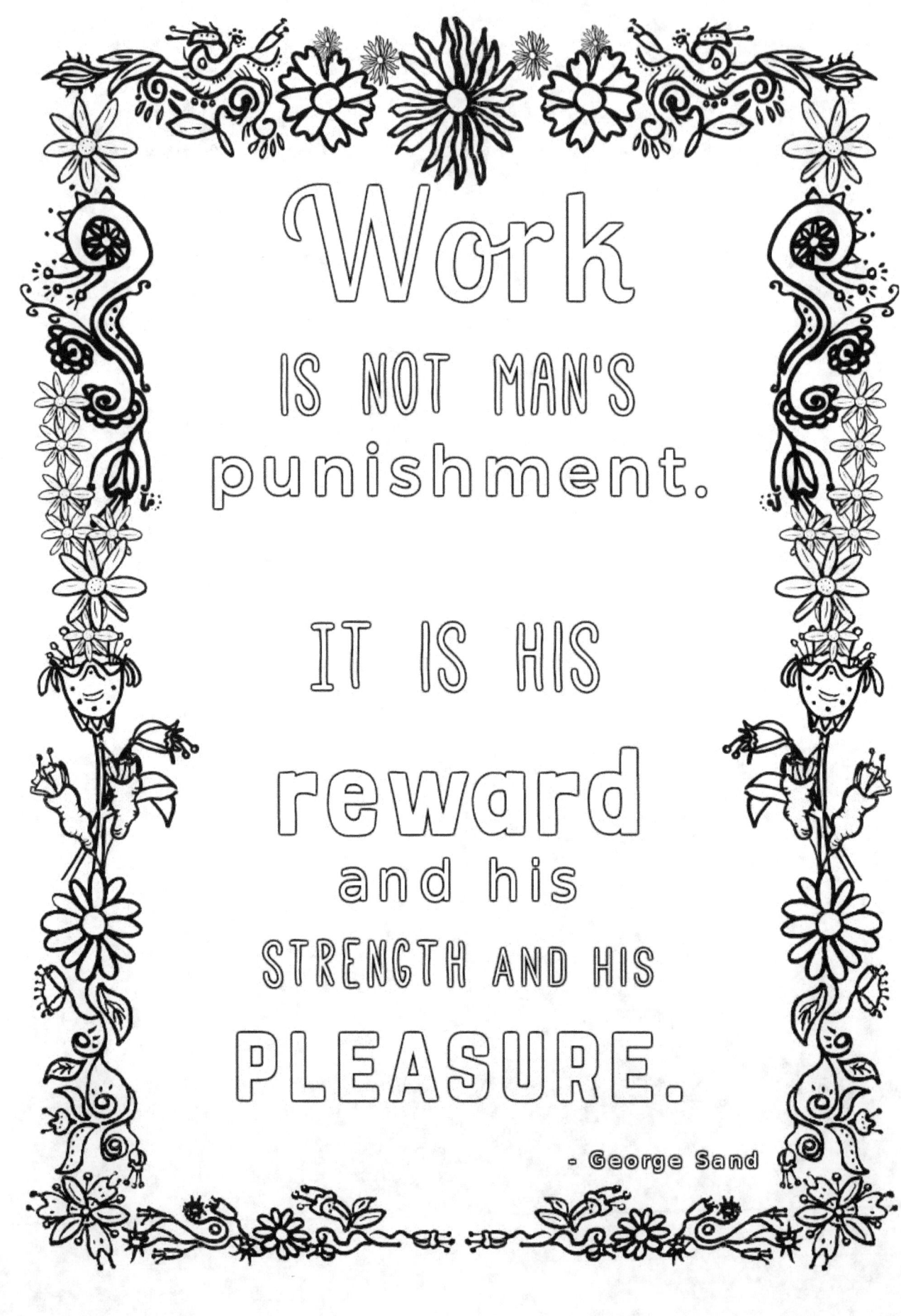

Work
IS NOT MAN'S
punishment.

IT IS HIS
reward
and his
STRENGTH AND HIS
PLEASURE.

- George Sand

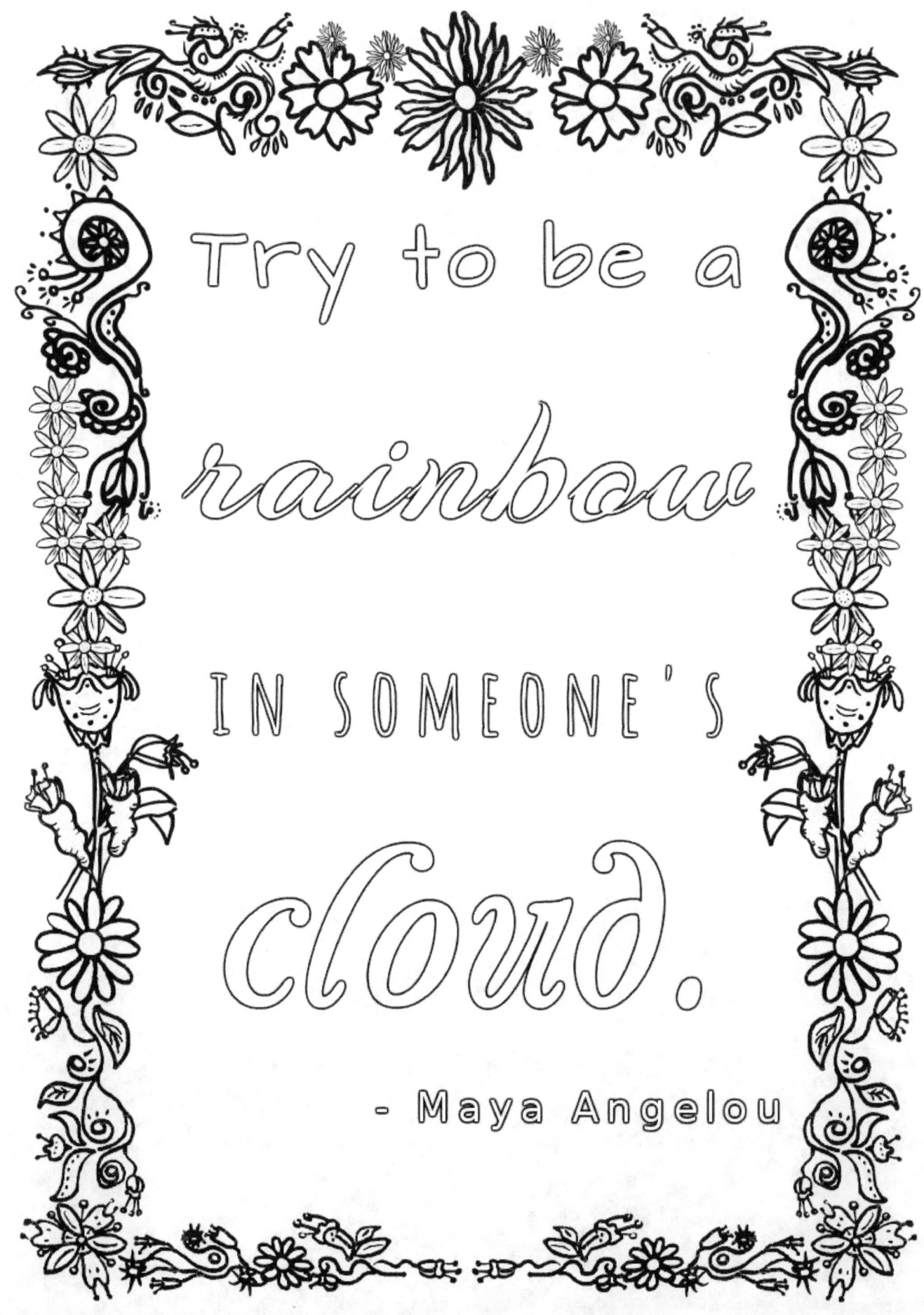

Try to be a

rainbow

IN SOMEONE'S

cloud.

- Maya Angelou

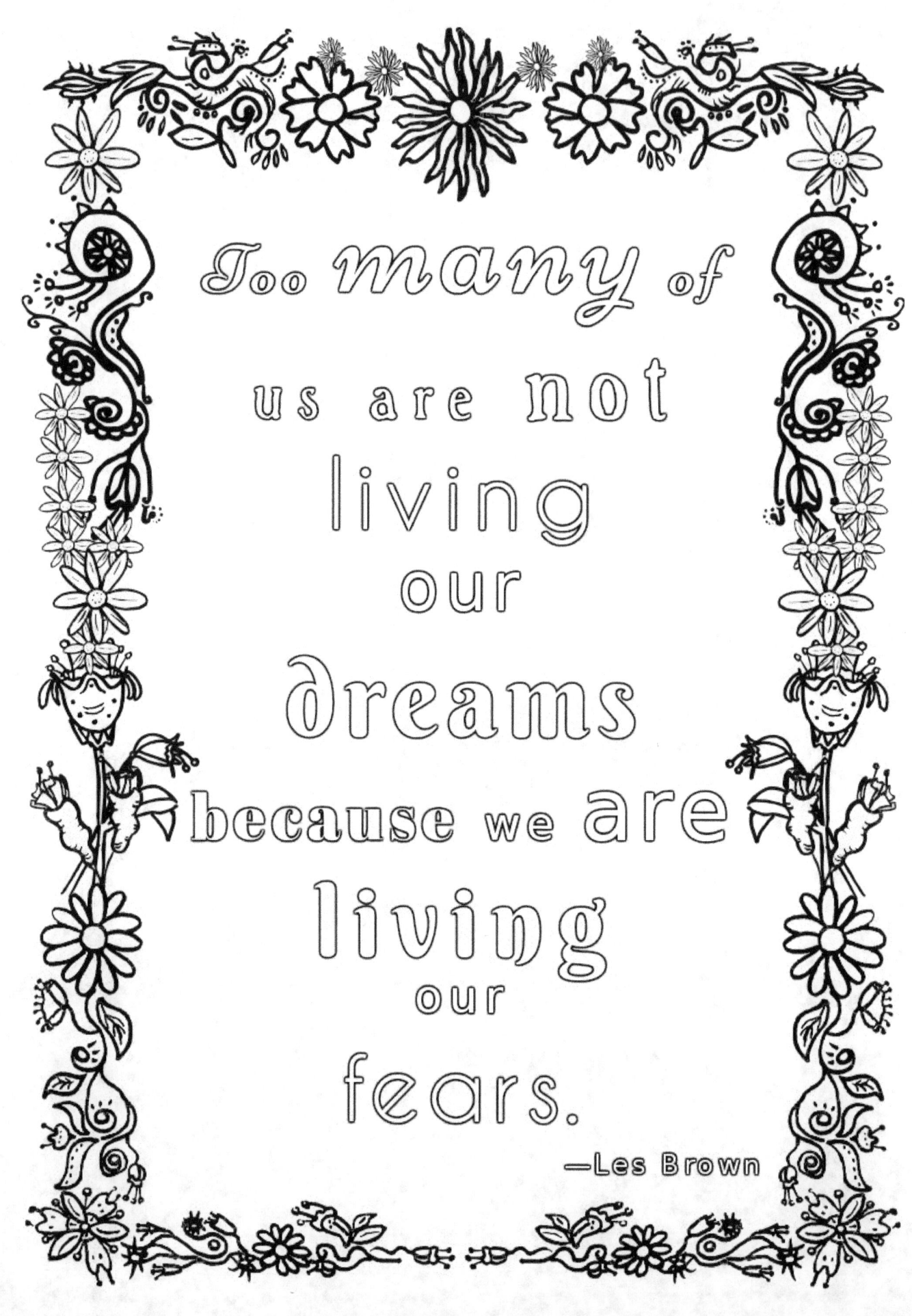

Too many of us are not living our dreams because we are living our fears.

—Les Brown

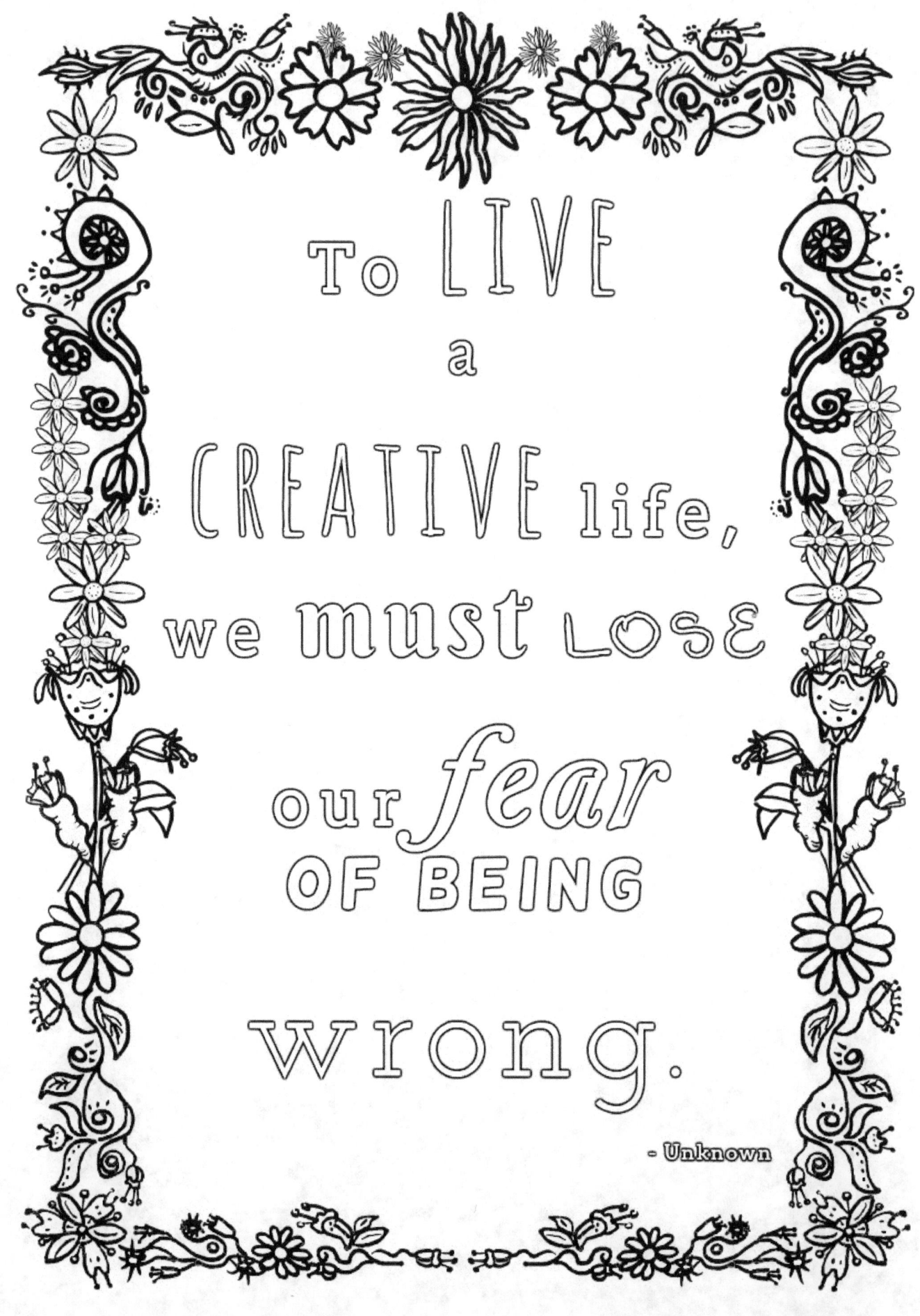

To LIVE a CREATIVE life, we must LOSE our *fear* OF BEING wrong.

- Unknown

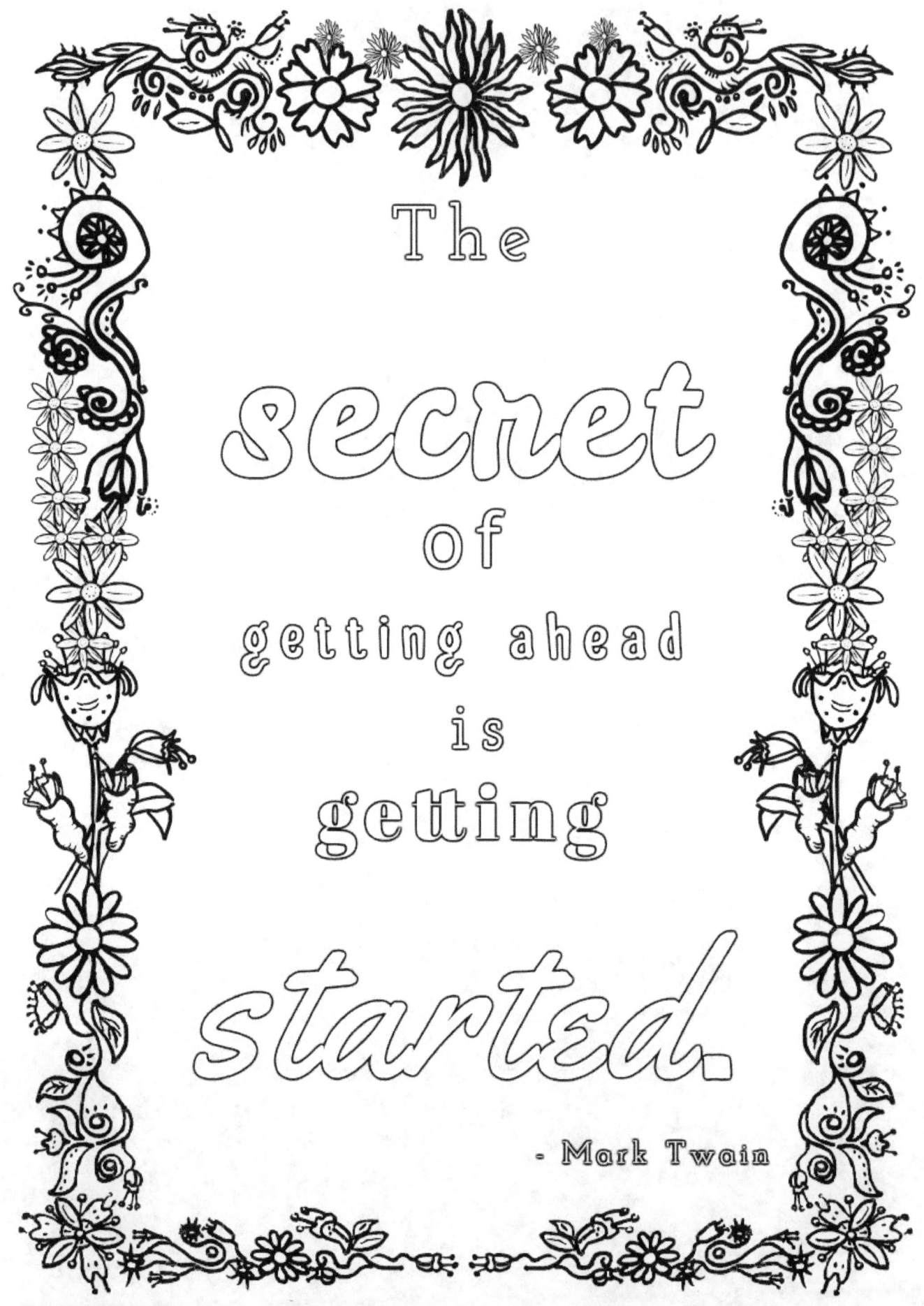

The **secret** of getting ahead is getting **started.**

- Mark Twain

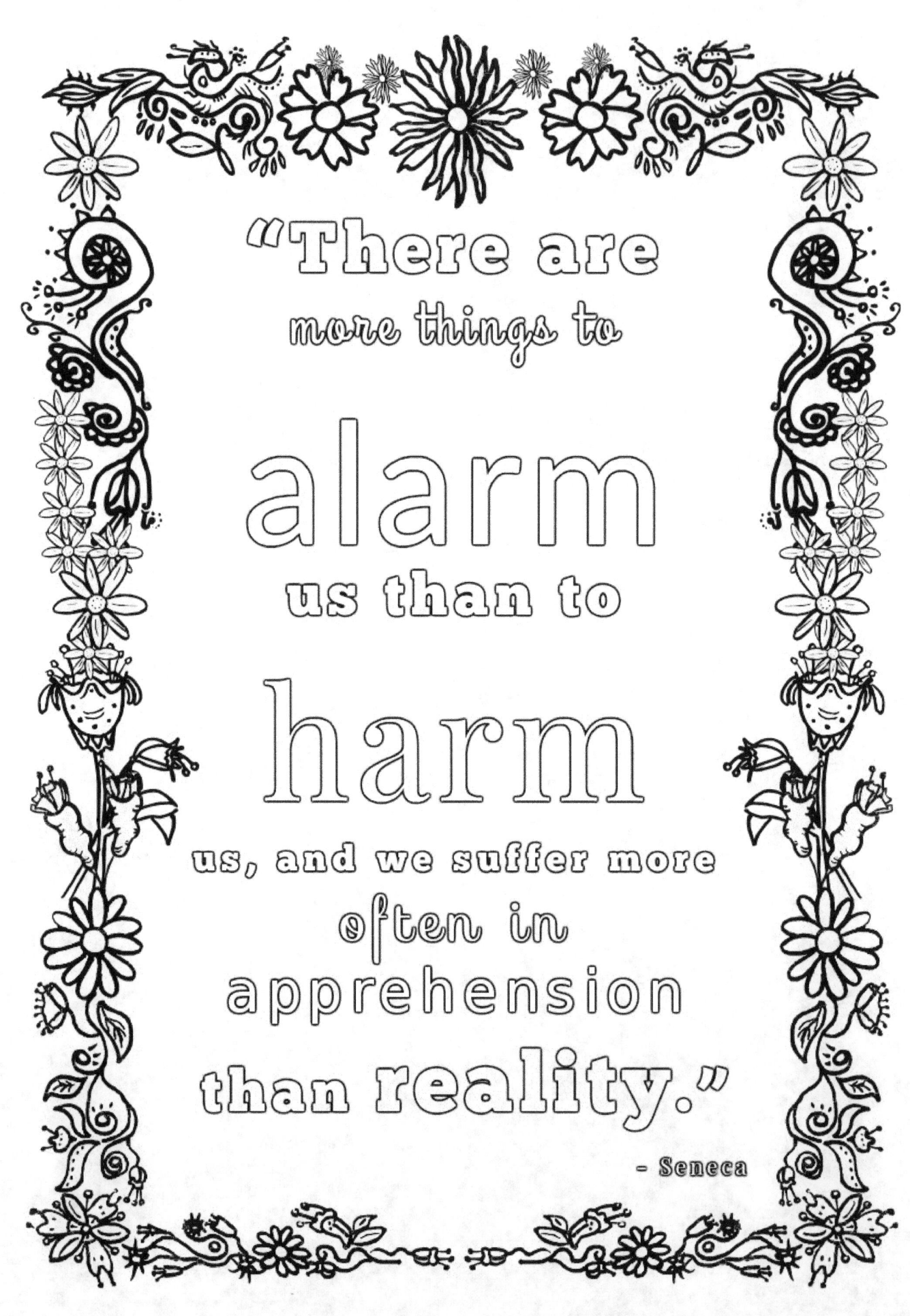

"There are more things to alarm us than to harm us, and we suffer more often in apprehension than reality."

— Seneca

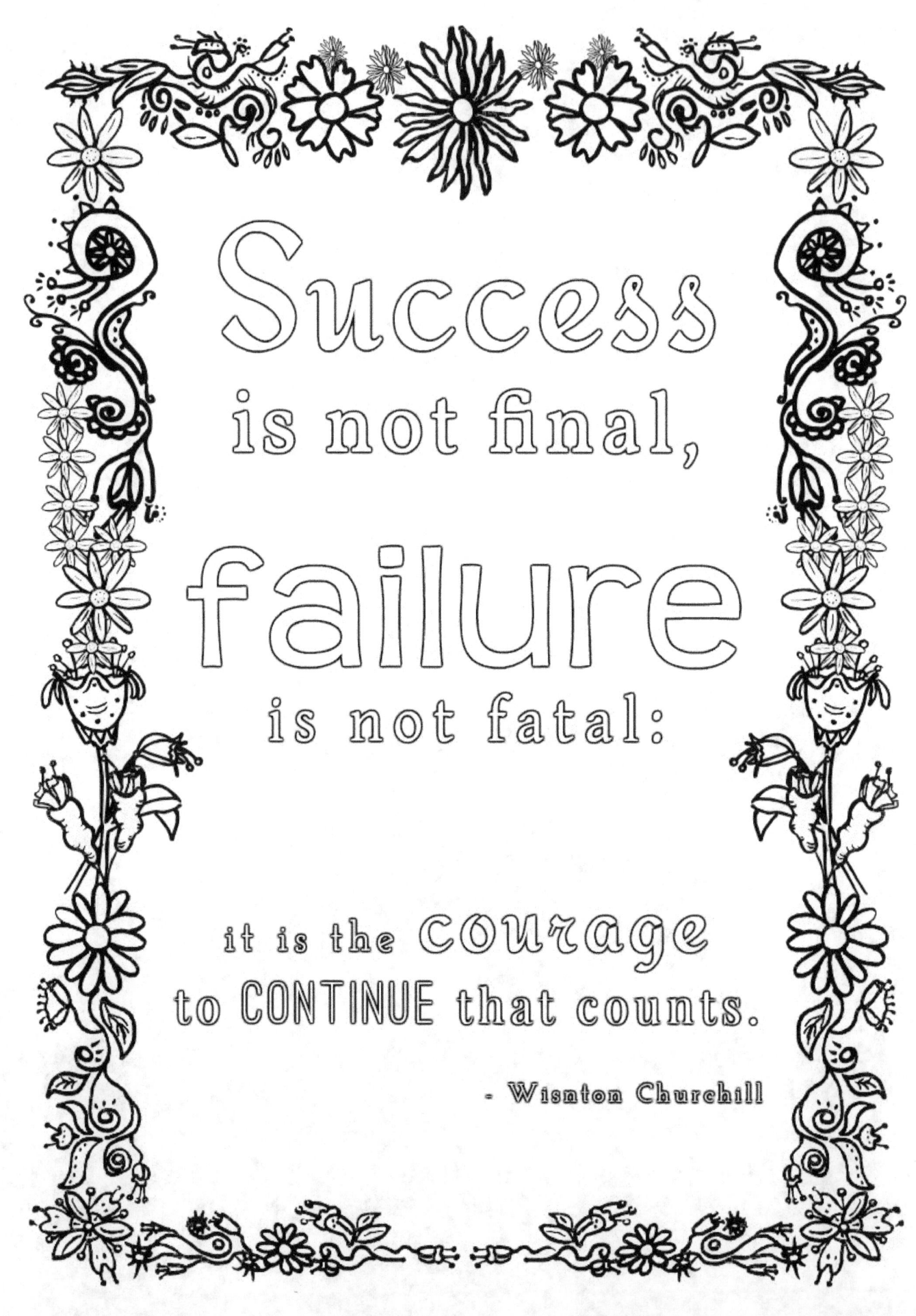

Success is not final, failure is not fatal: it is the COURAGE to CONTINUE that counts.

- Wisnton Churchill

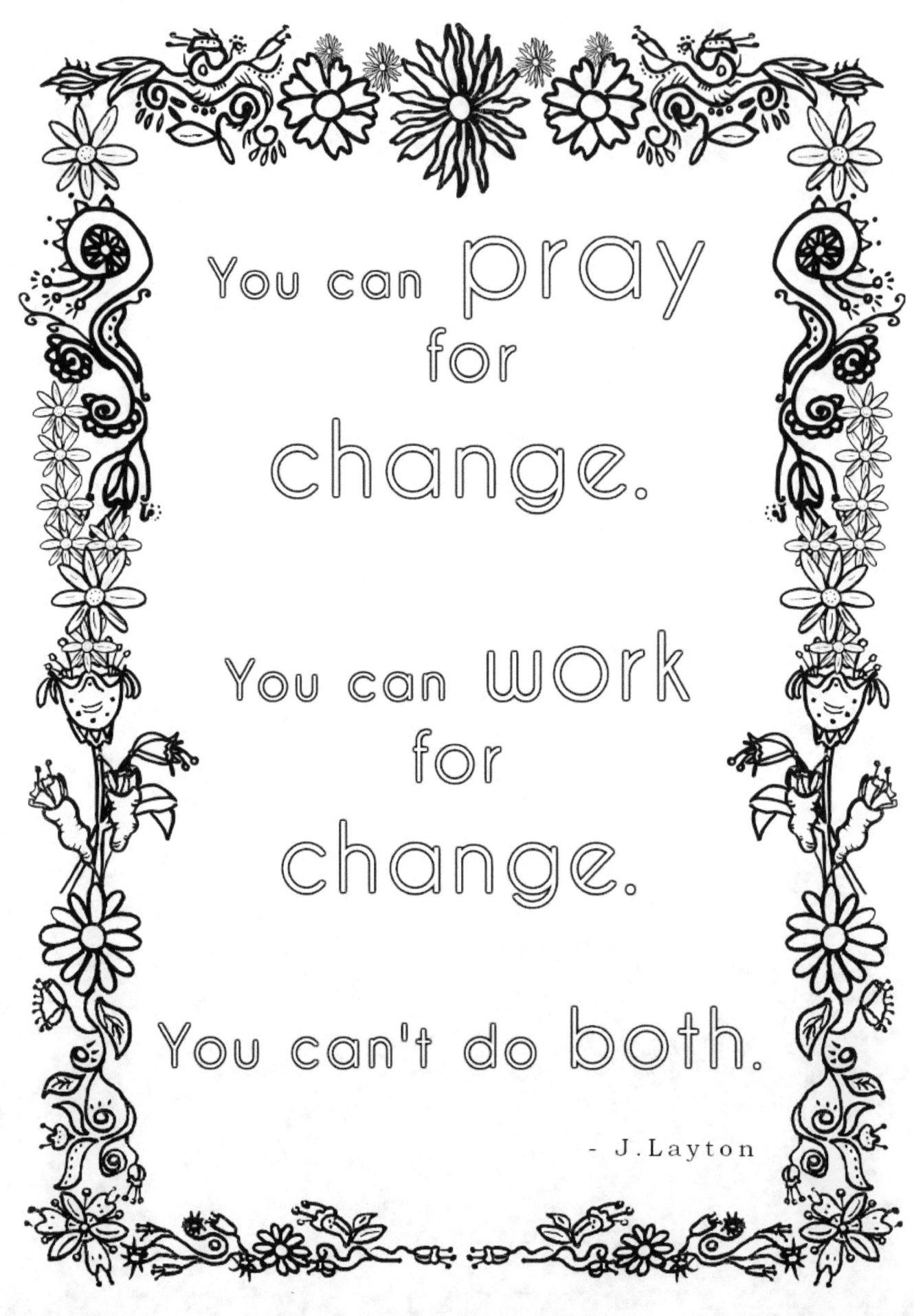

You can **pray** for change.

You can **work** for change.

You can't do both.

— J. Layton

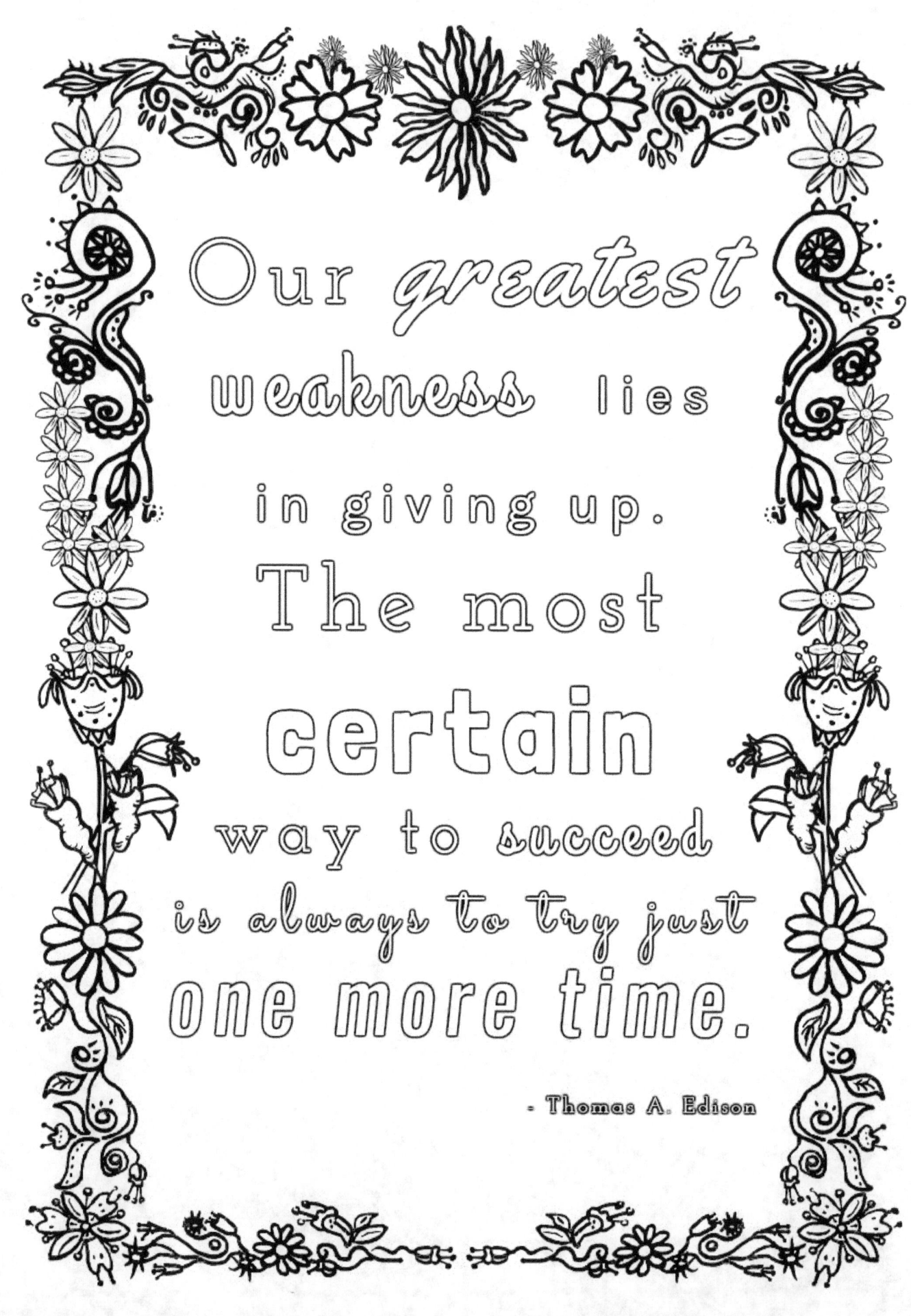

Our *greatest* weakness lies in giving up. The most certain way to succeed is always to try just one more time.

- Thomas A. Edison

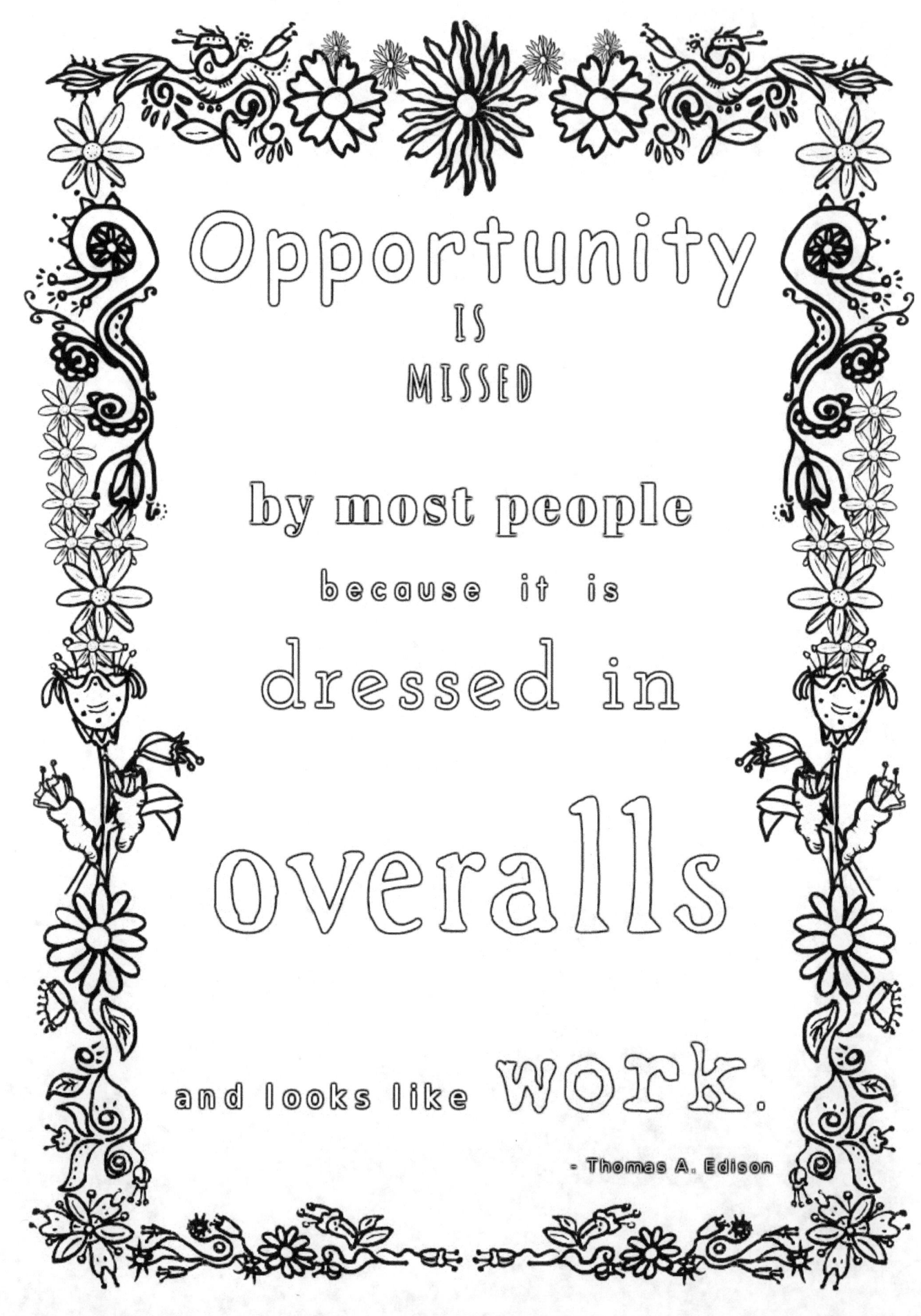

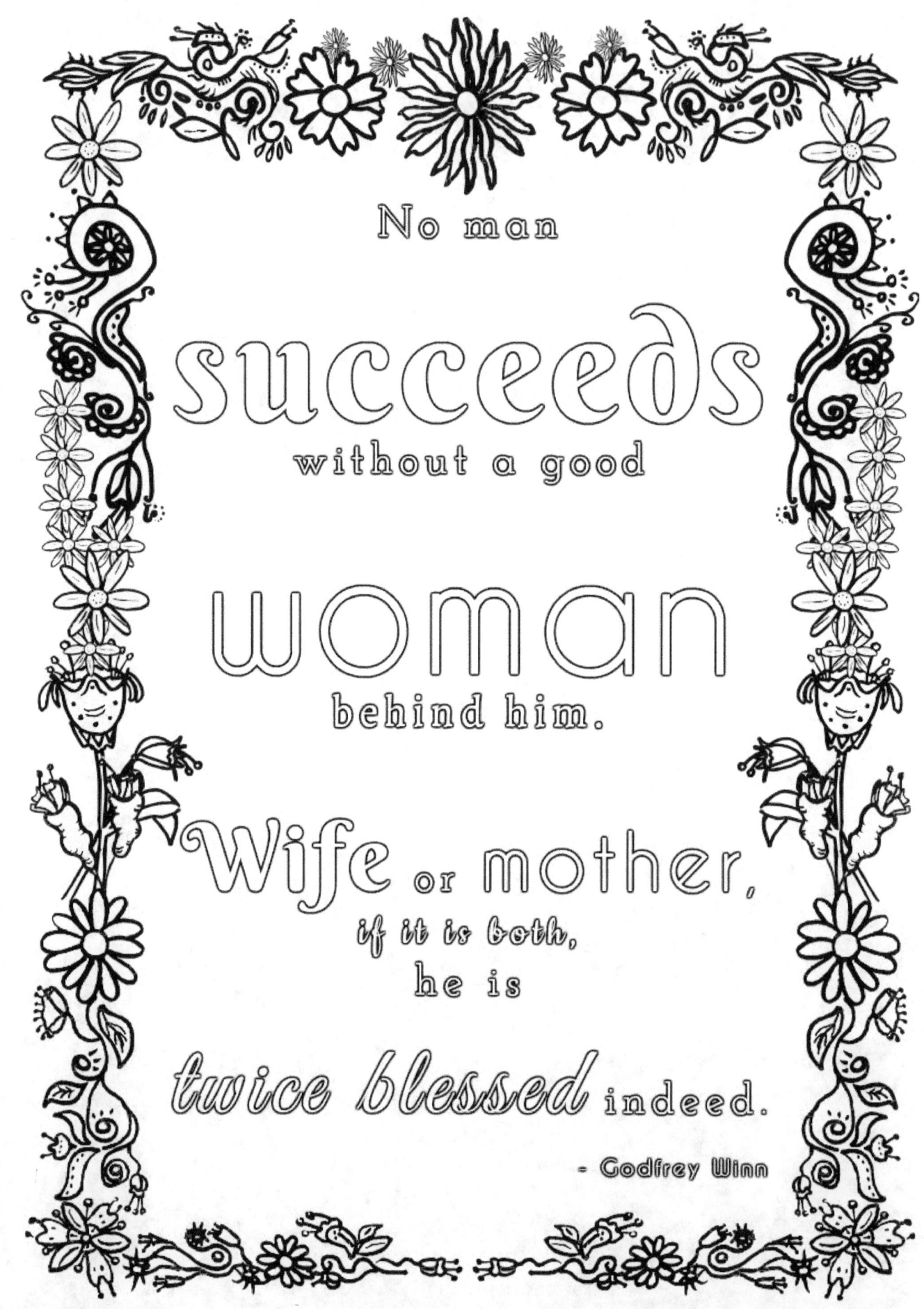

No man
succeeds
without a good
woman
behind him.
Wife or mother,
if it is both,
he is
twice blessed indeed.

— Godfrey Winn

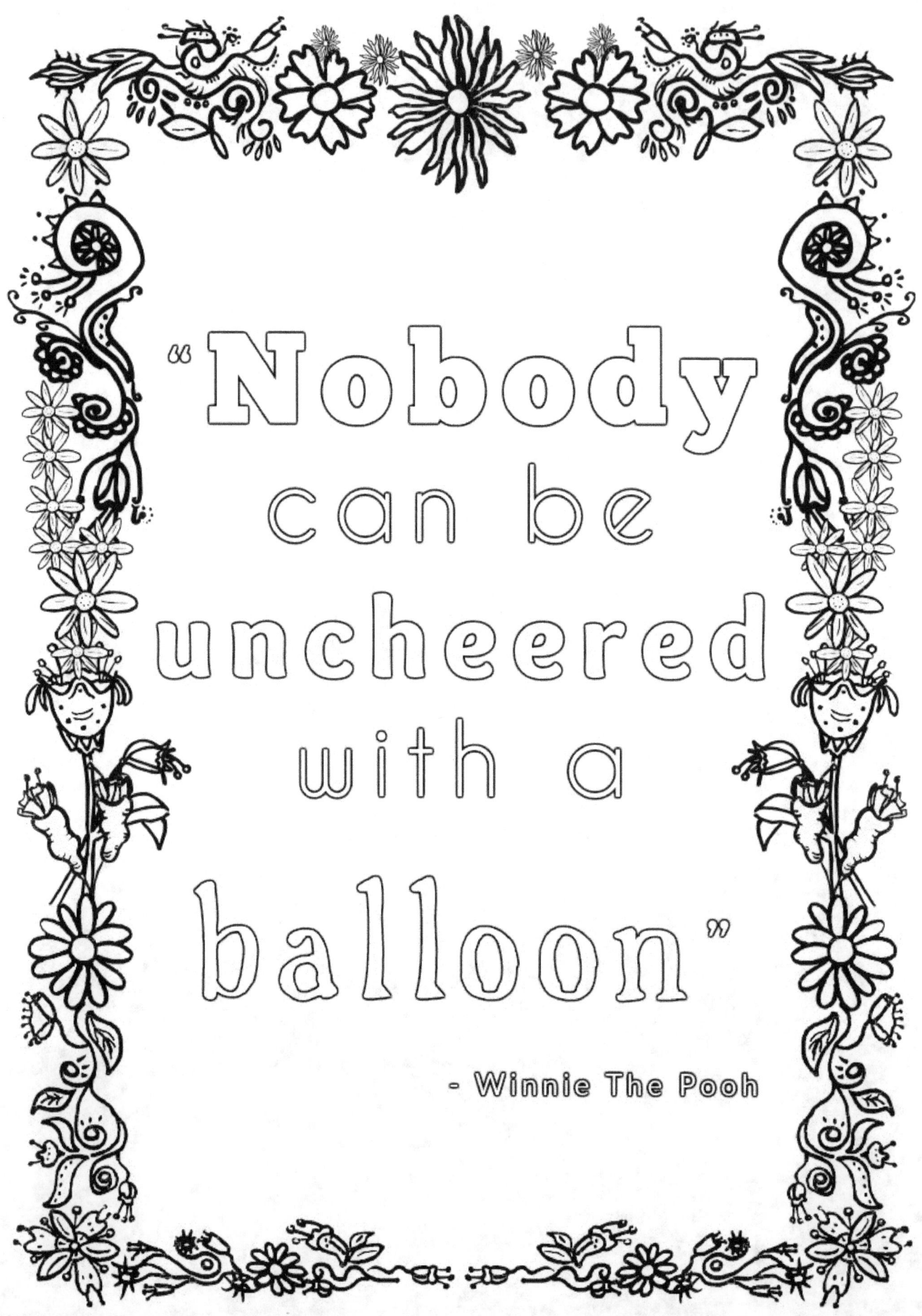

"Nobody can be uncheered with a balloon"

- Winnie The Pooh

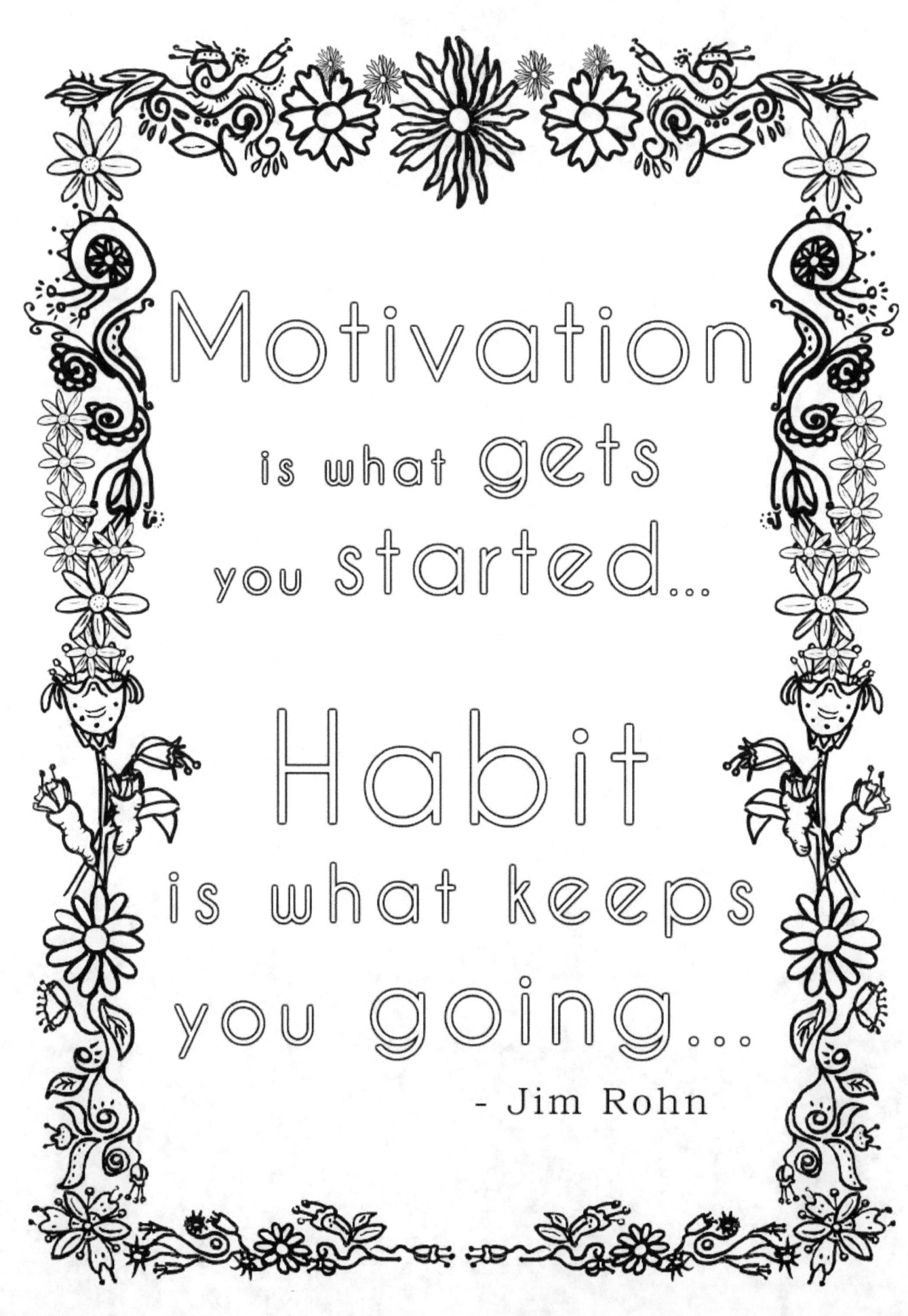

Motivation is what gets you started...

Habit is what keeps you going...

- Jim Rohn

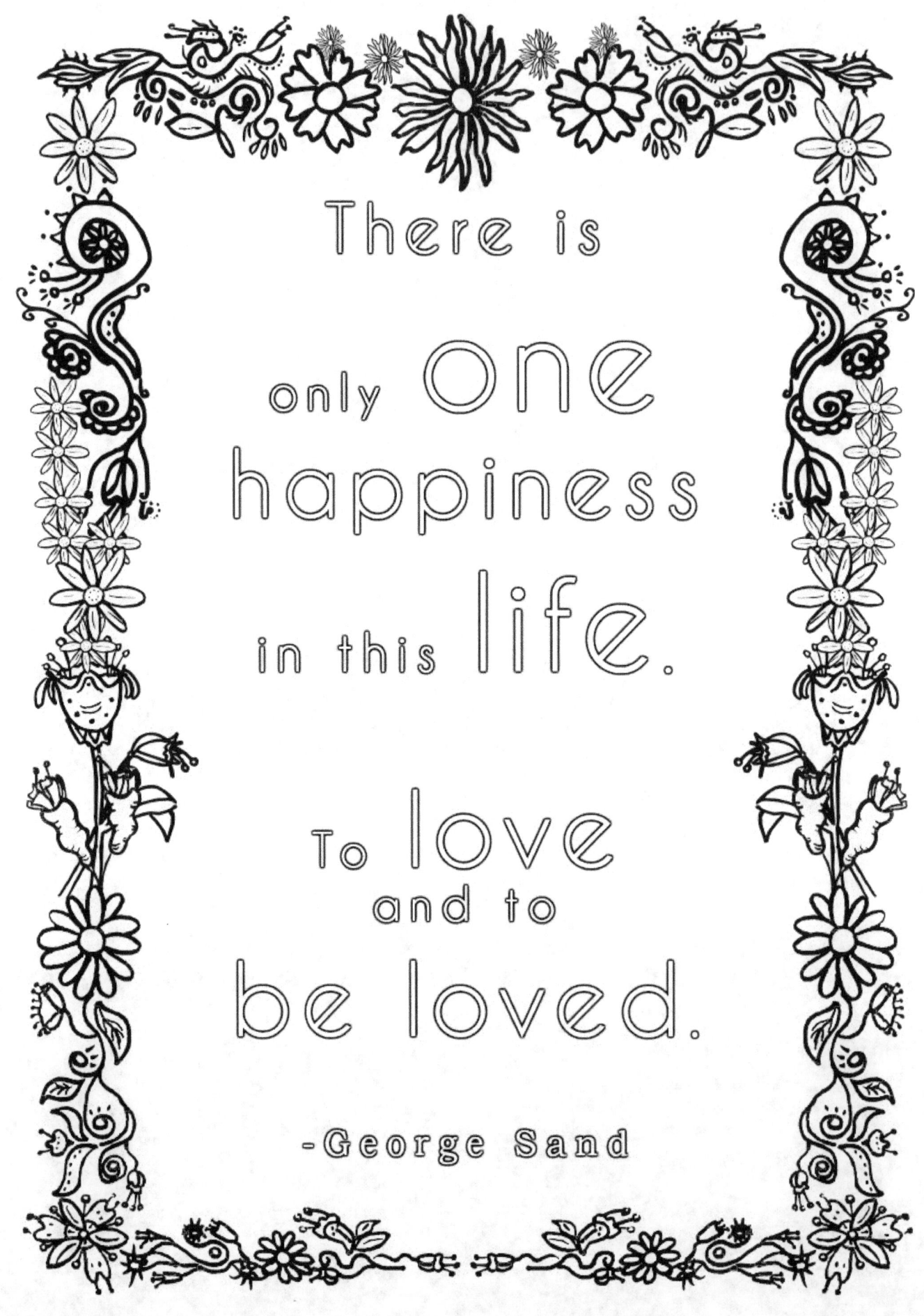

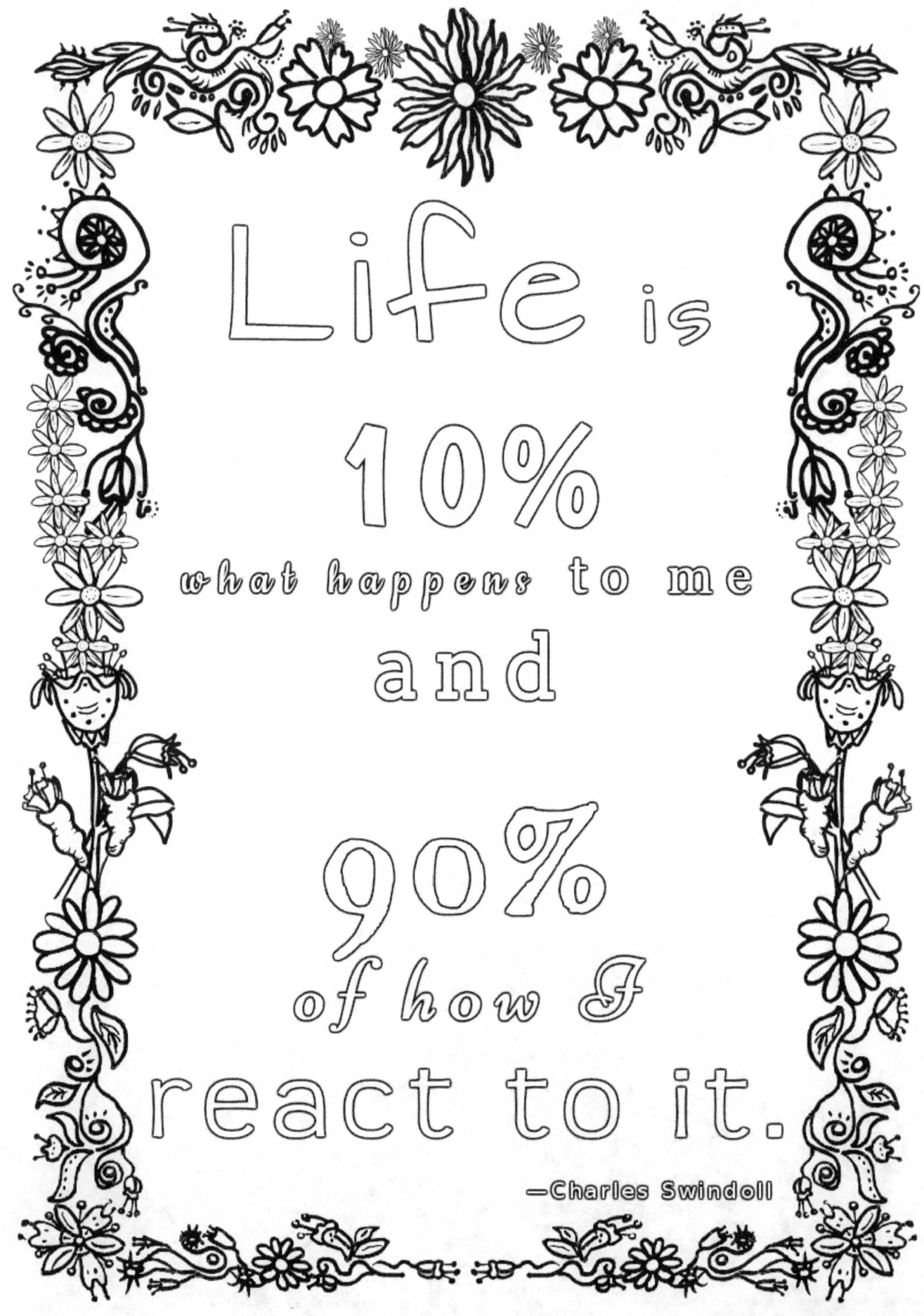

Life is
10%
what happens to me
and
90%
of how I
react to it.
—Charles Swindoll

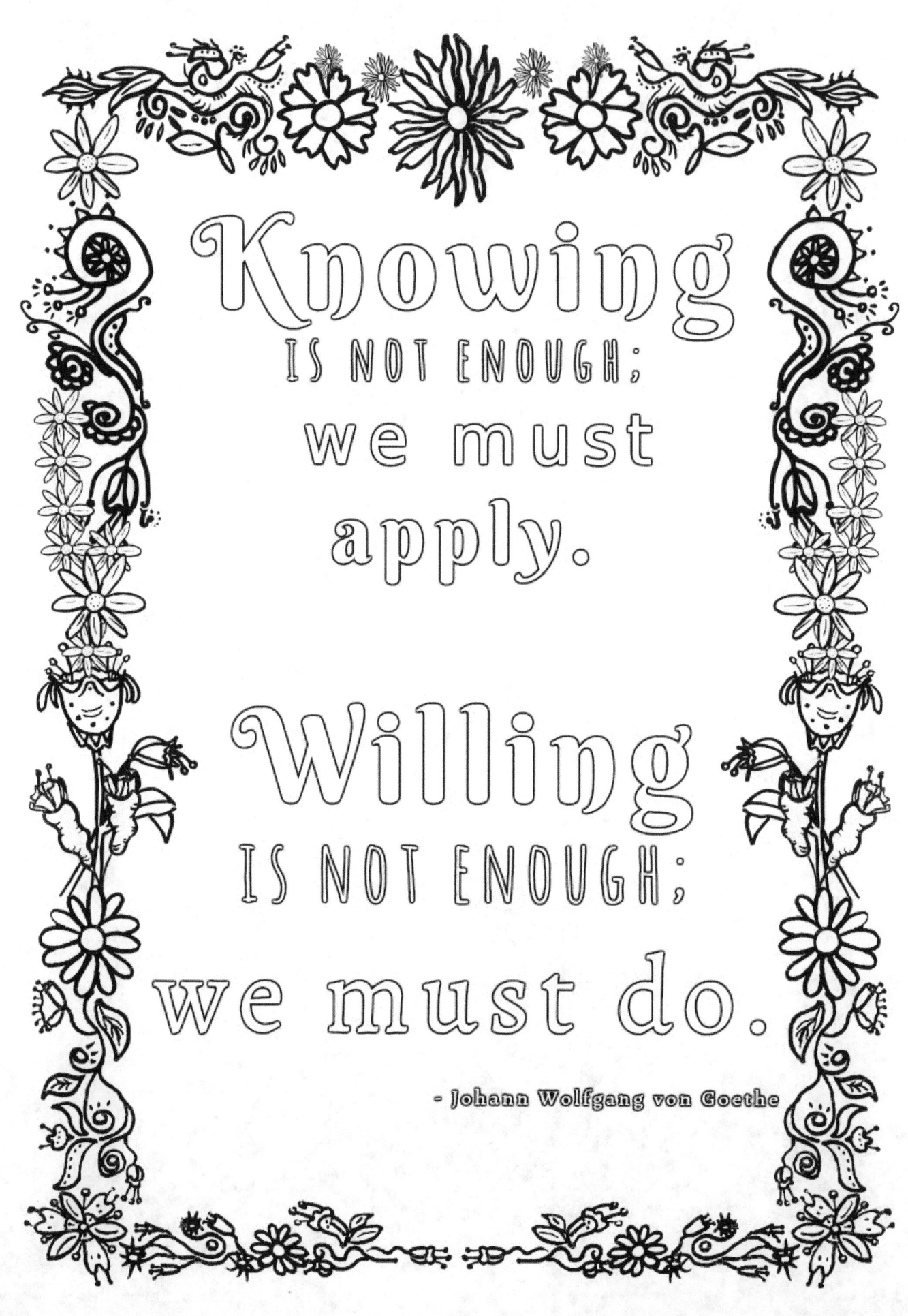

Knowing
IS NOT ENOUGH;
we must
apply.

Willing
IS NOT ENOUGH;
we must do.

- Johann Wolfgang von Goethe

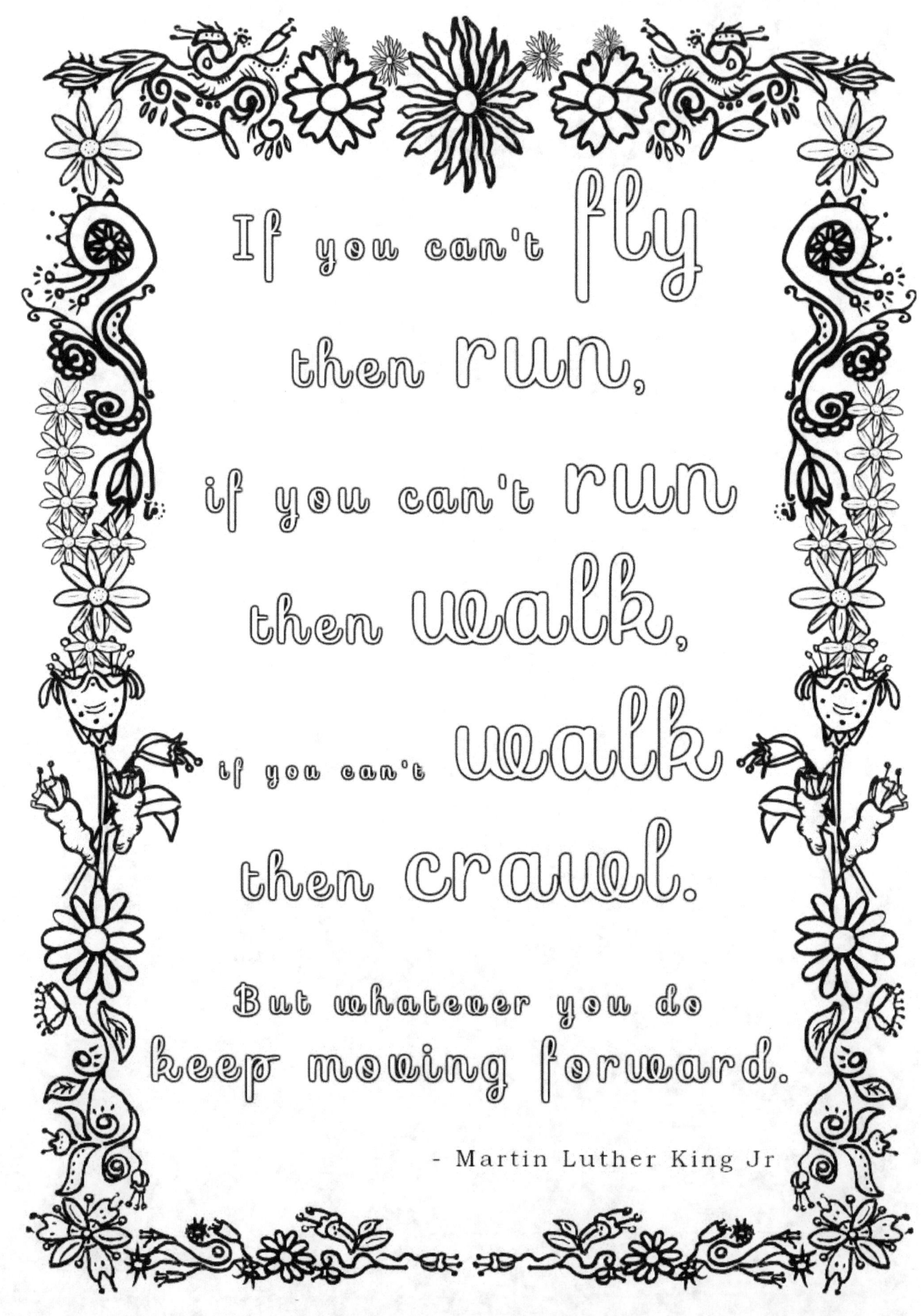

If you can't **fly**
then **run**,
if you can't **run**
then **walk**,
if you can't **walk**
then **crawl**.

But whatever you do
keep moving forward.

- Martin Luther King Jr

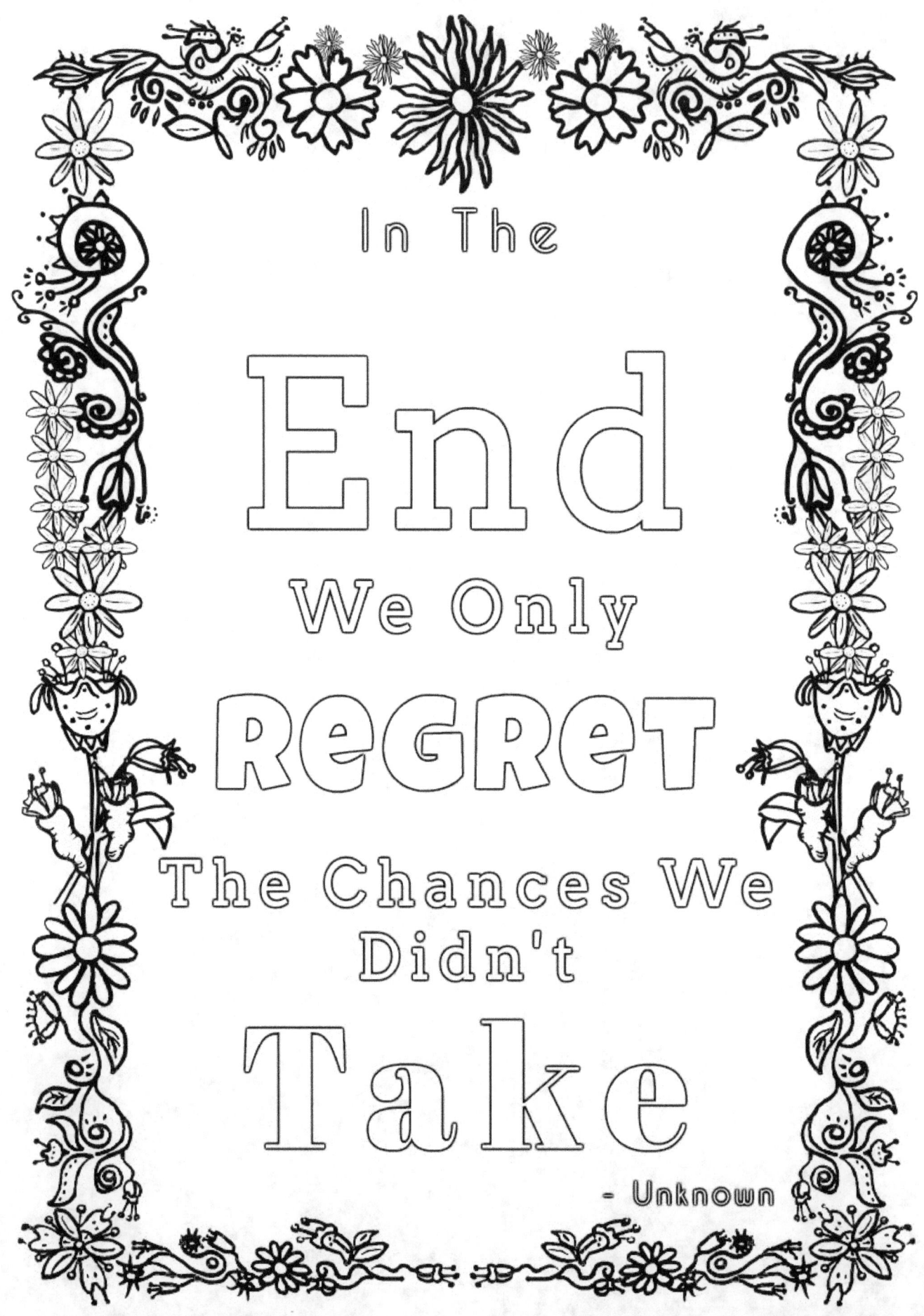

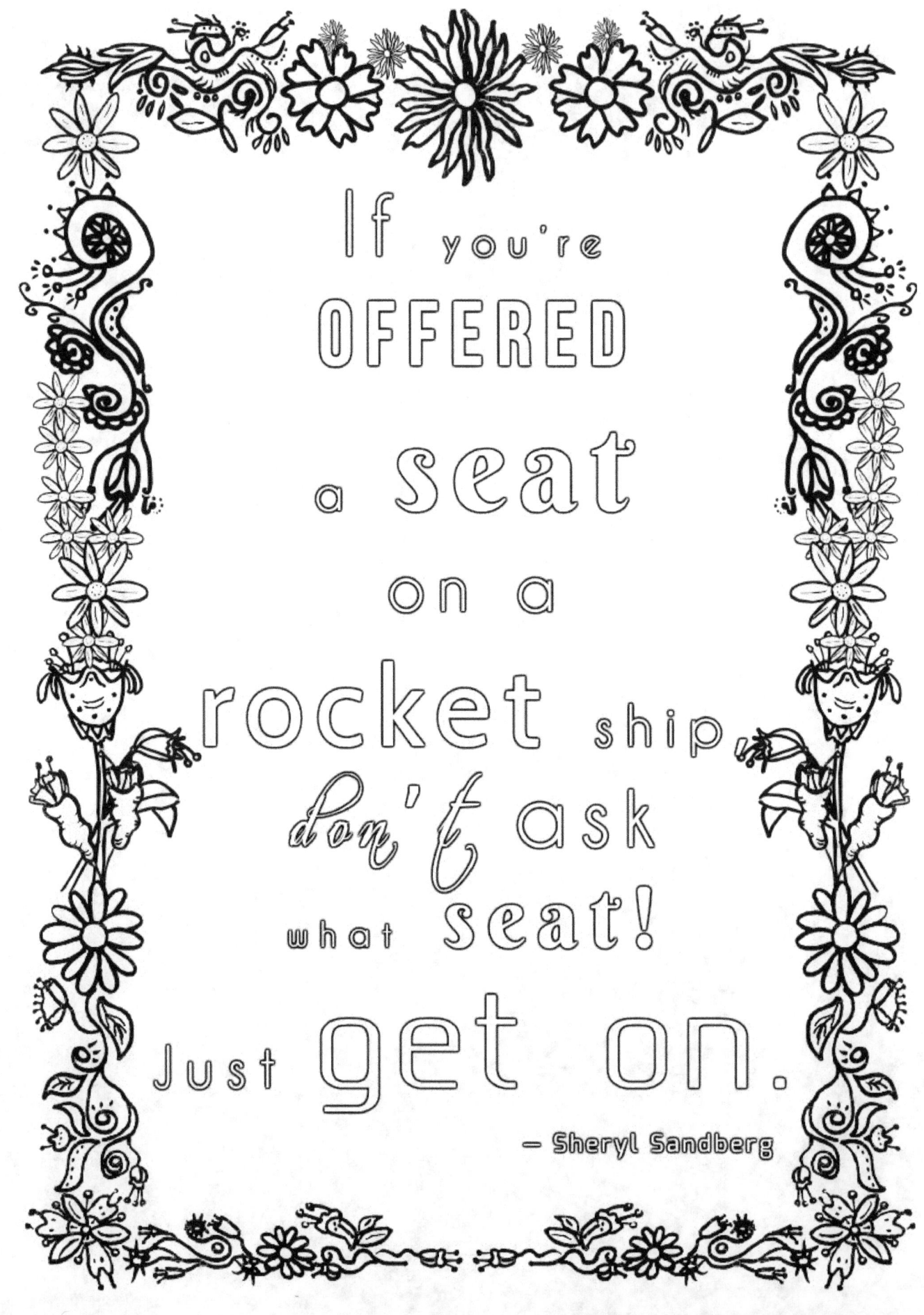

If you're OFFERED a seat on a rocket ship, don't ask what seat! Just get on.

— Sheryl Sandberg

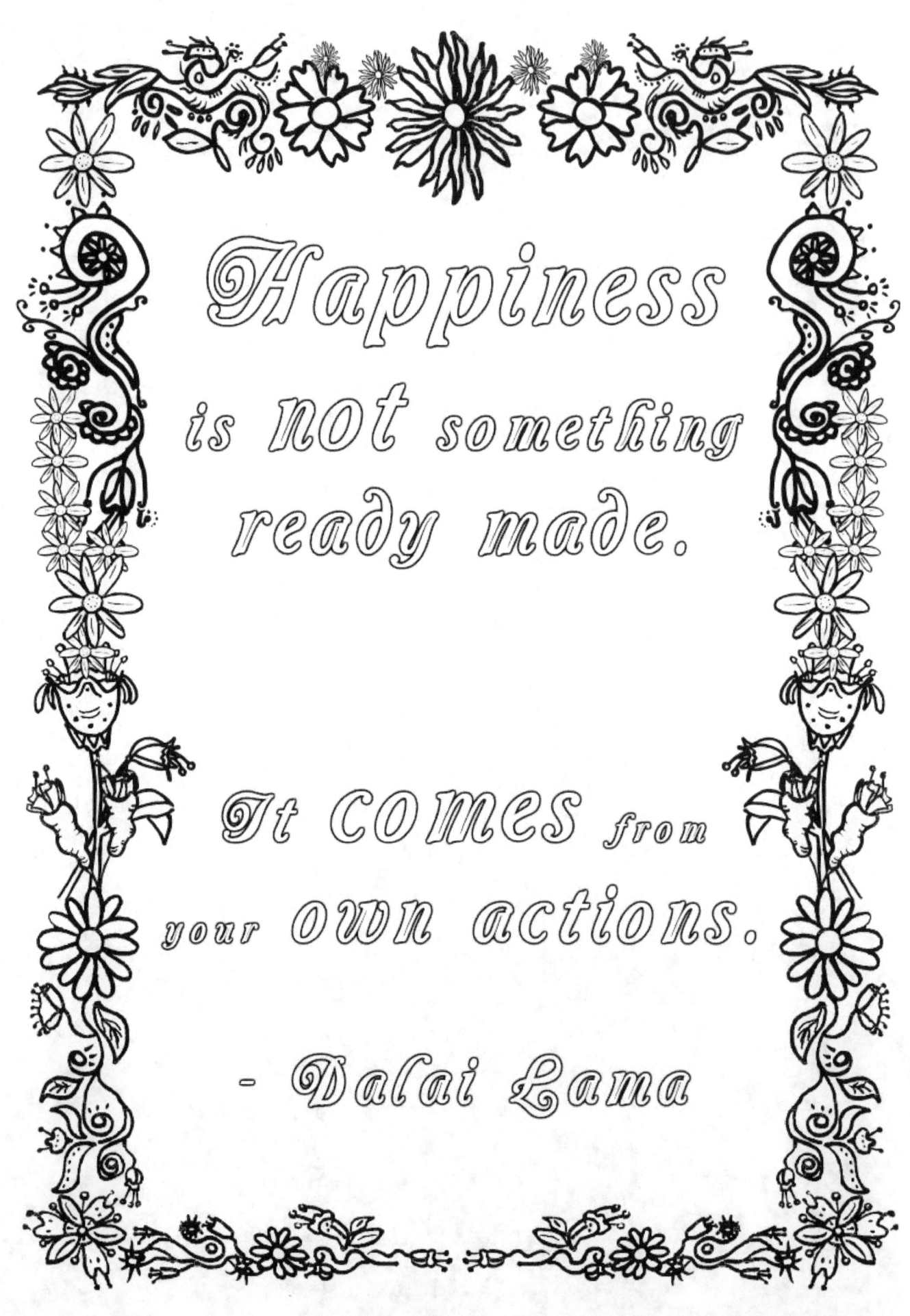

Happiness is not something ready made. It comes from your own actions.

- Dalai Lama

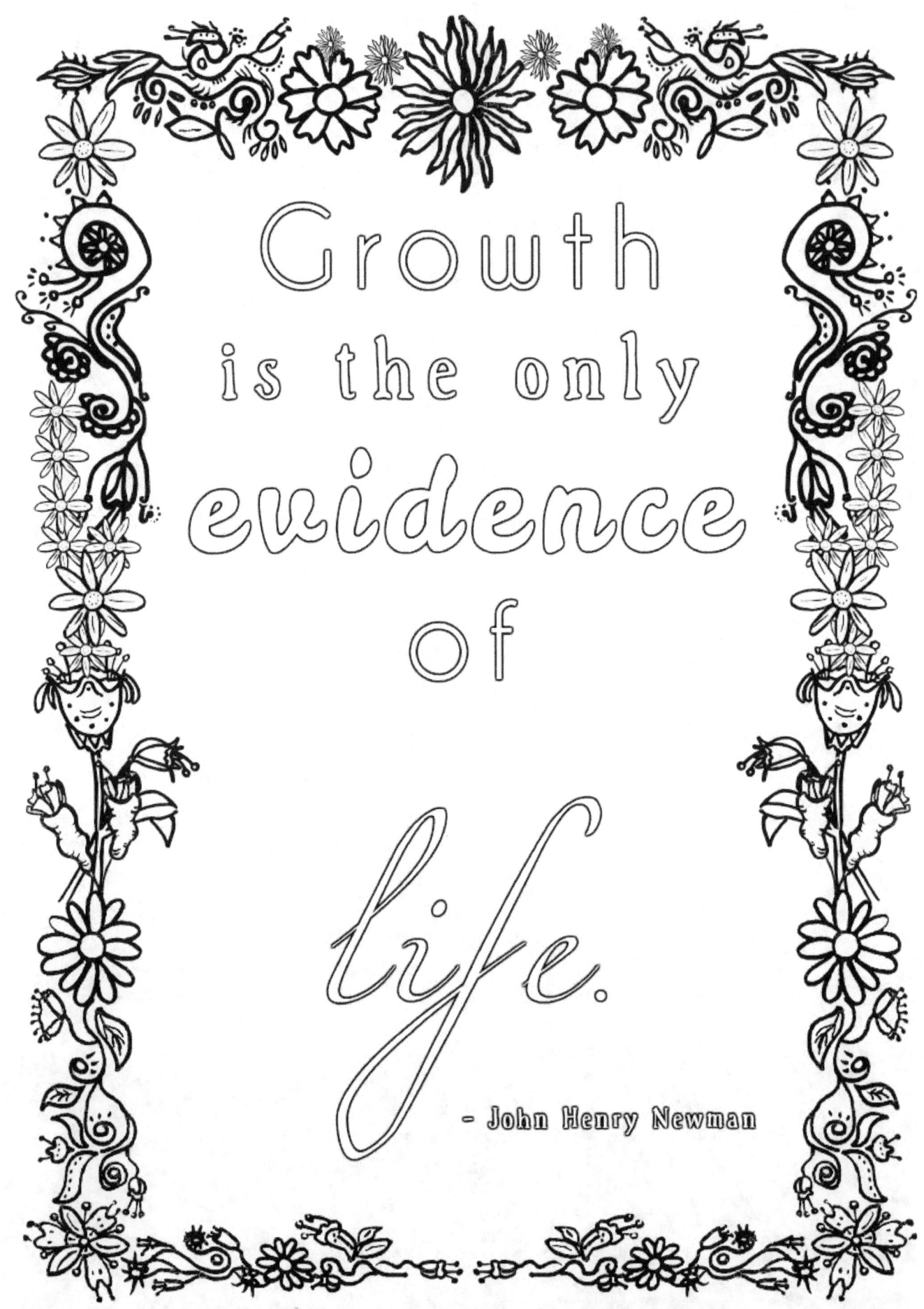

Growth is the only evidence of life.

— John Henry Newman

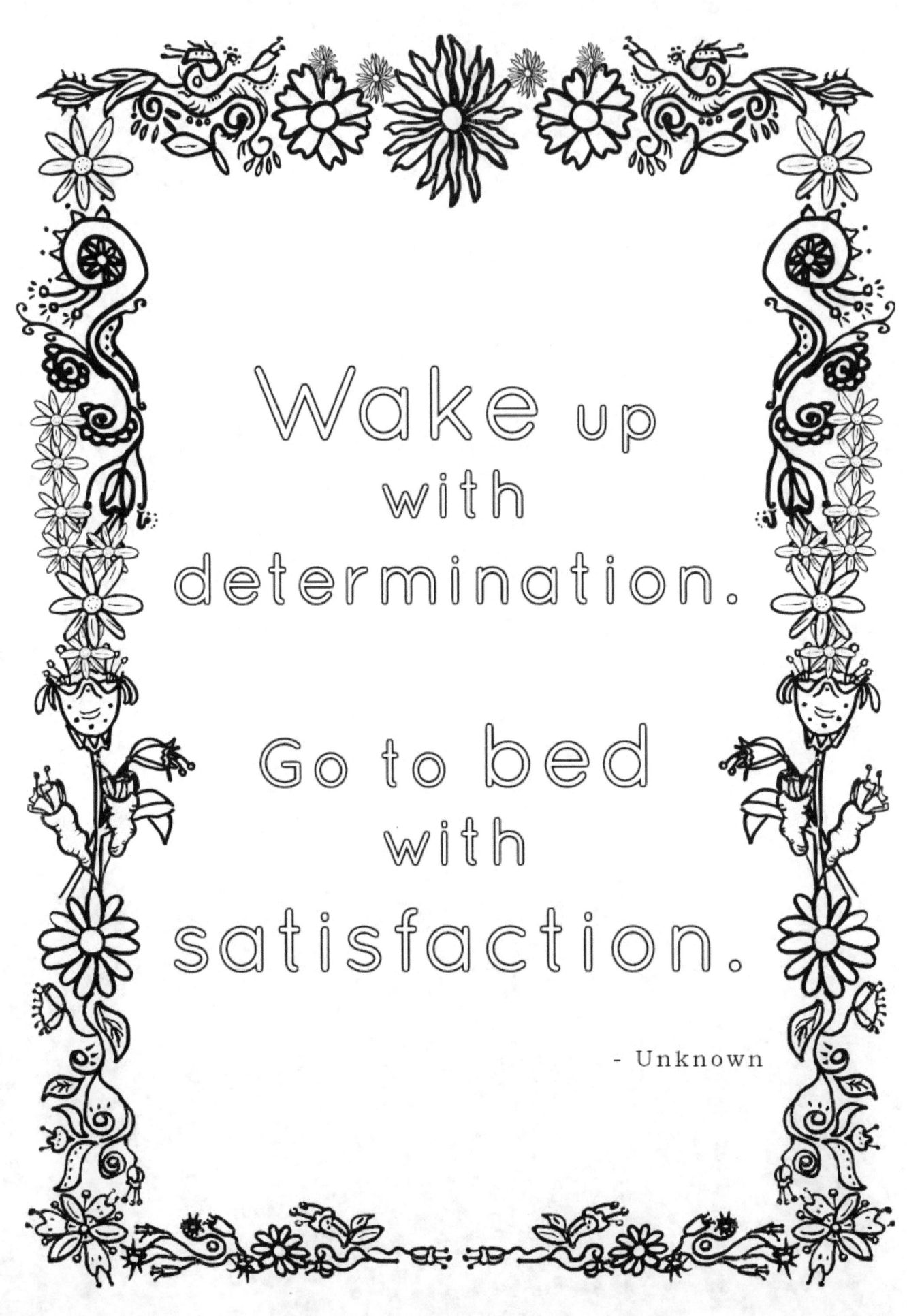

Wake up
with
determination.

Go to bed
with
satisfaction.

- Unknown

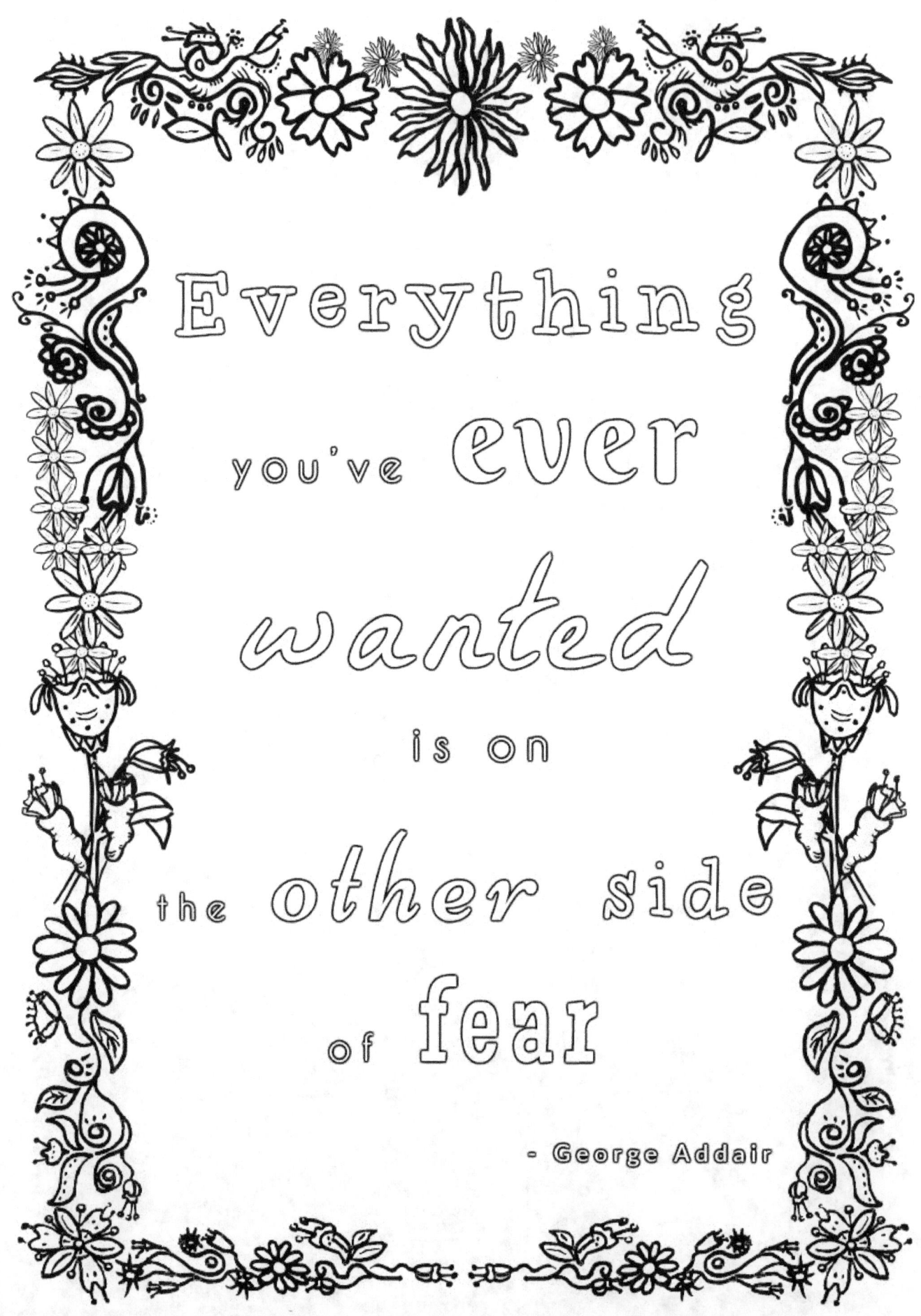

Everything you've ever wanted is on the other side of fear

- George Addair

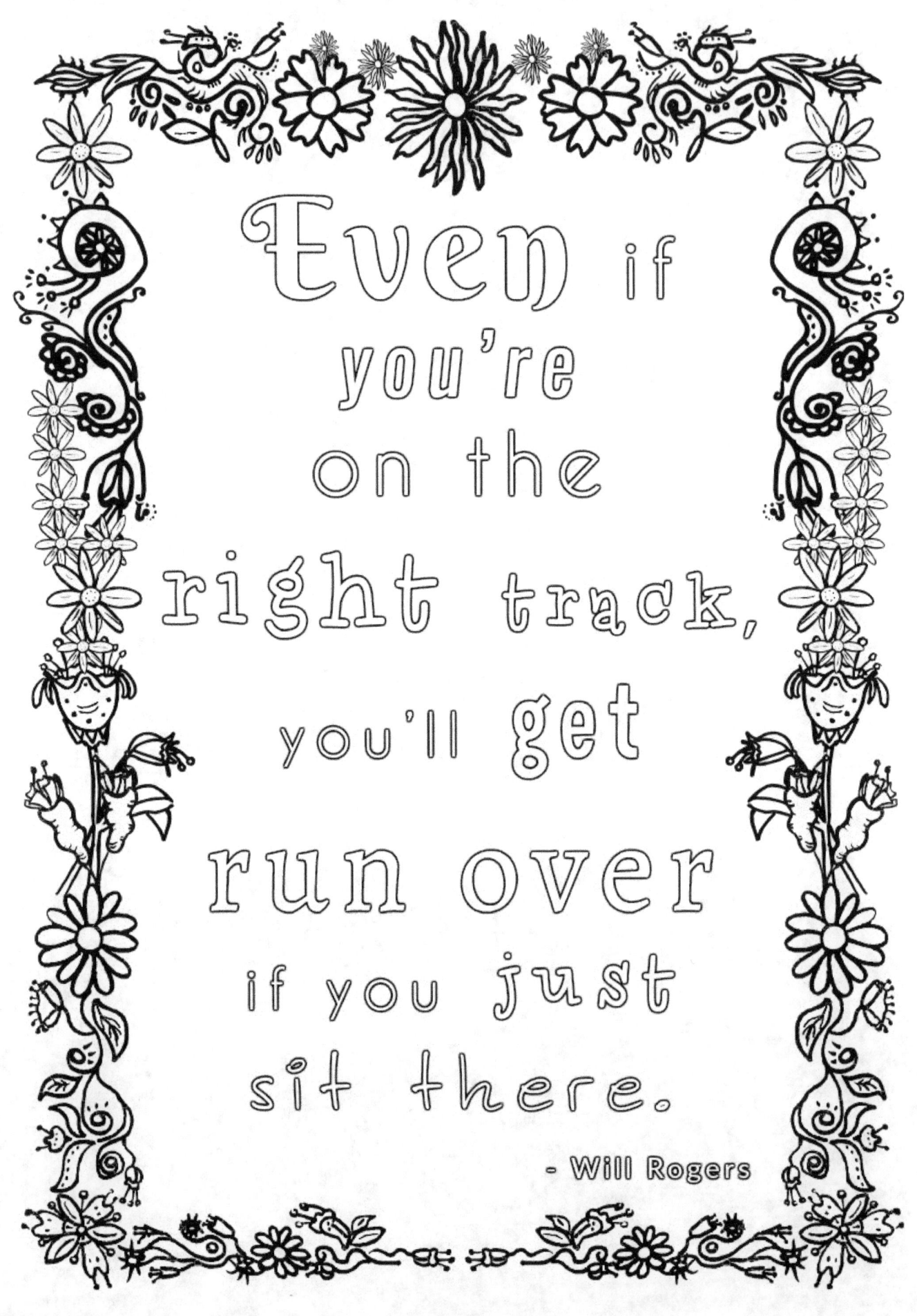

Even if you're on the right track, you'll get run over if you just sit there.

- Will Rogers

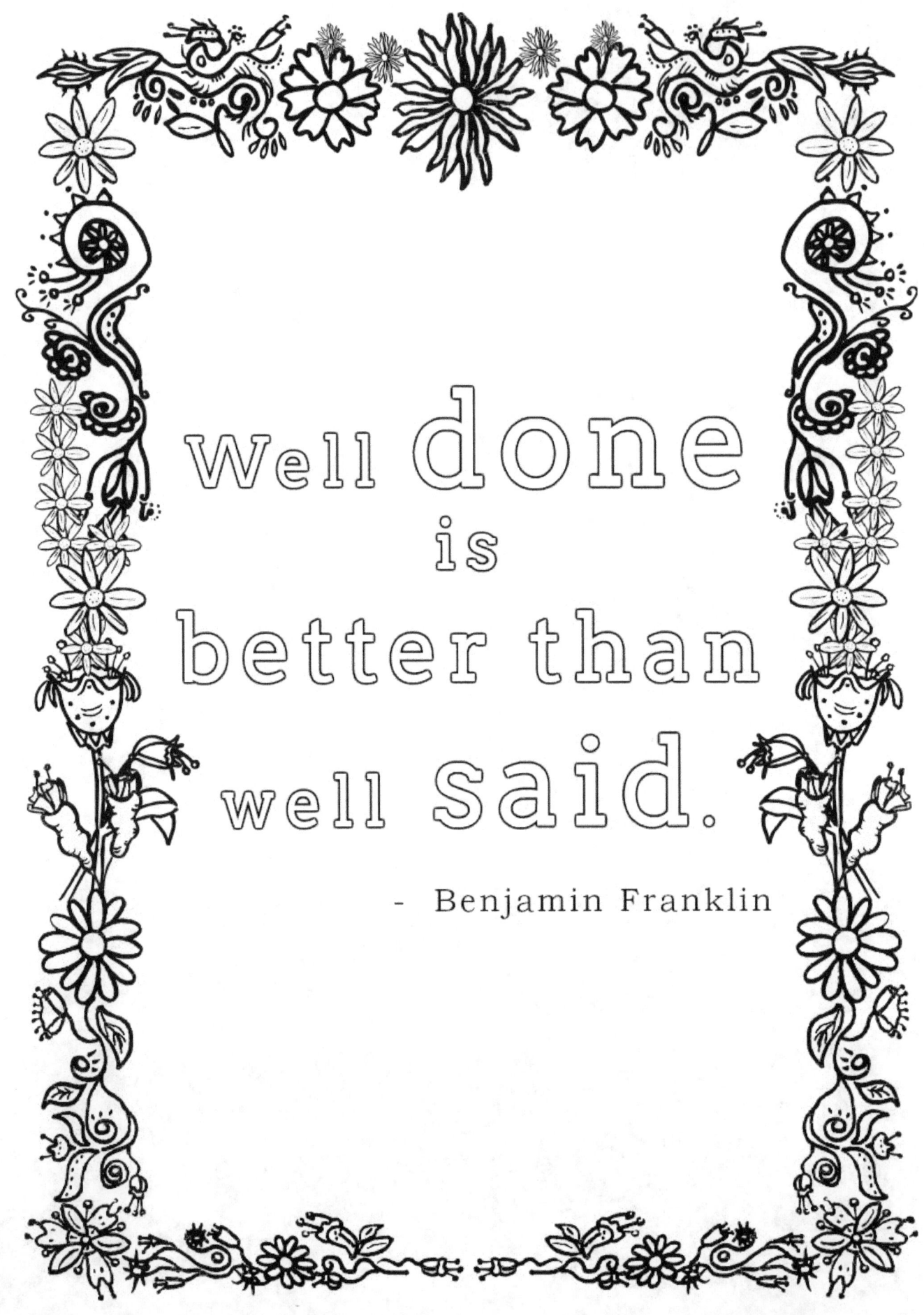

Well done
is
better than
well said.

- Benjamin Franklin

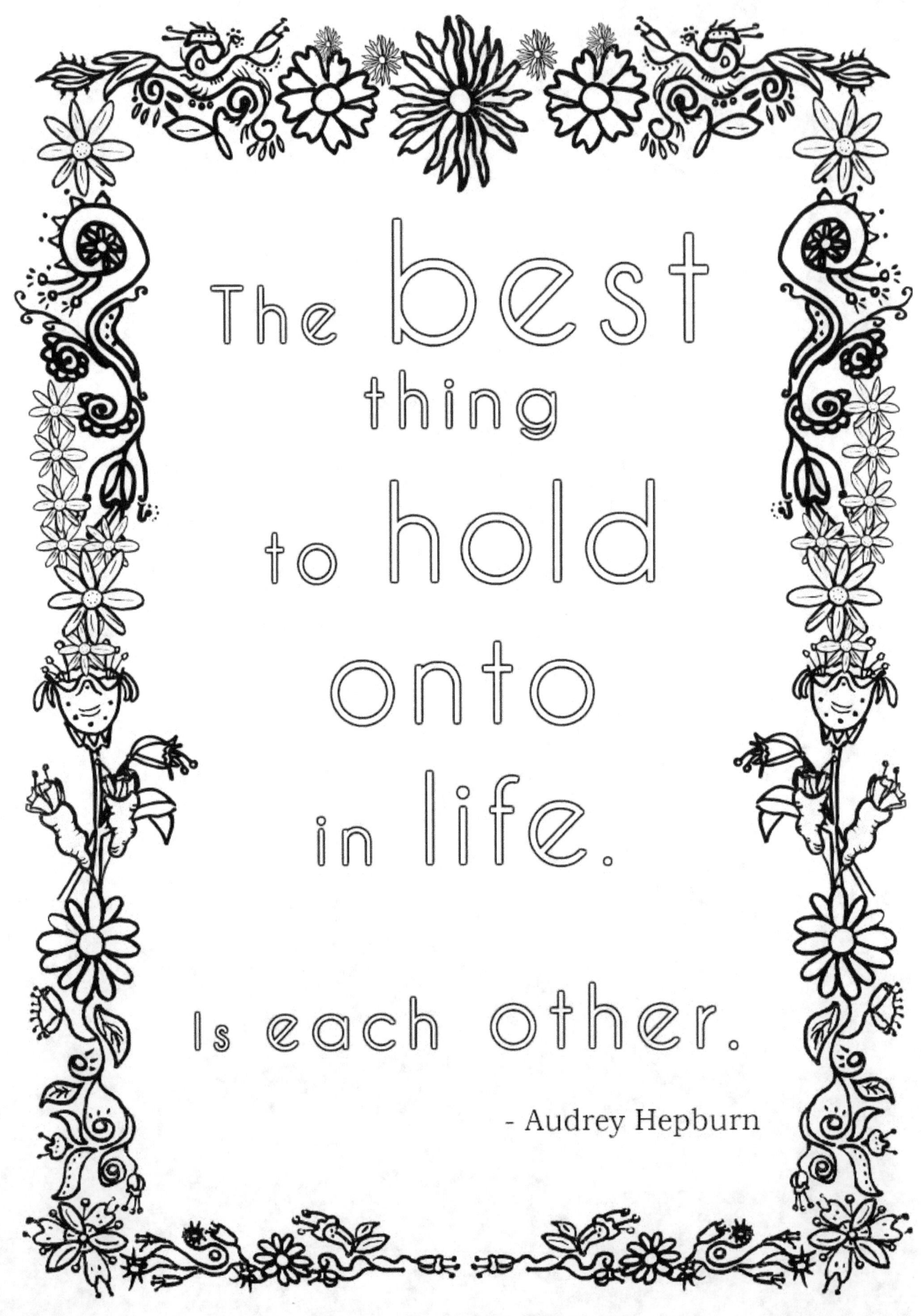

The best
thing
to hold
onto
in life.

Is each other.

- Audrey Hepburn

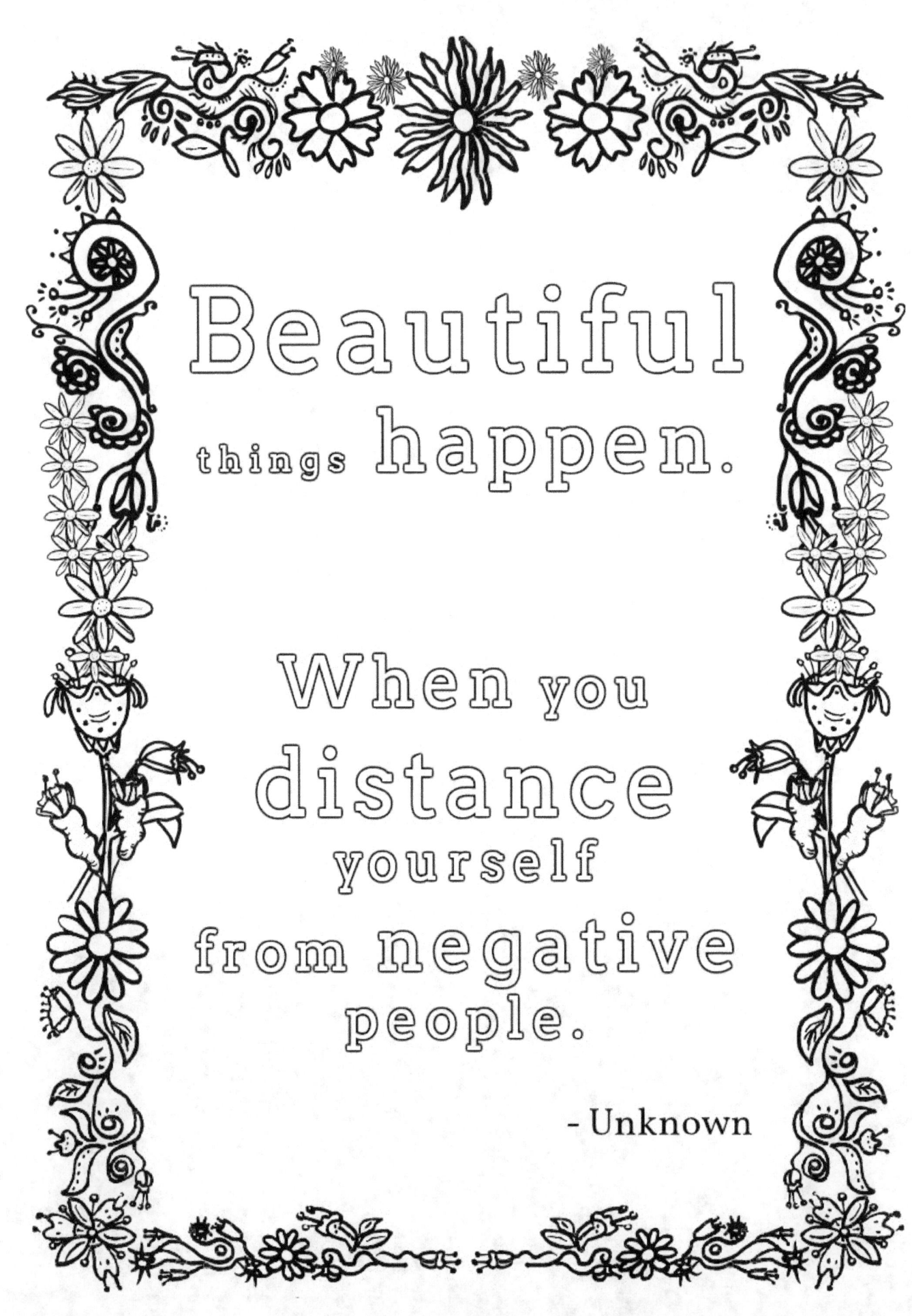

Beautiful things happen.

When you distance yourself from negative people.

- Unknown

Hi, I know you have things going on today but could you do something for me? Leaving a review helps others find good coloring books and lets the world know how YOU feel about this one.

Go on... please?

Leave a review?

stop by...

www.sprinklespublishing.com

...to get some freebies or just see what else we do.

Or

...scan this with your phone to win a free book!!

Sprinkles Publishing

"Lose Yourself In A World Of Color"

Sprinkles Publishing CO.

10 Lyndon Croft

B37 7EW

United Kingdom